Want free goodies?
Email us at freebies@pbleu.com

@papeteriebleu

Papeterie Bleu

Shop our other books at
www.pbleu.com

Wholesale distribution through Ingram Content Group
www.ingramcontent.com/publishers/distribution/wholesale

For questions and customer service, email us at
support@pbleu.com

FREE PDF DOWNLOAD OF THIS BOOK

www.pbleu.com/adminlife

YOUR DOWNLOAD CODE: ADM373

 @papeteriebleu

 Papeterie Bleu

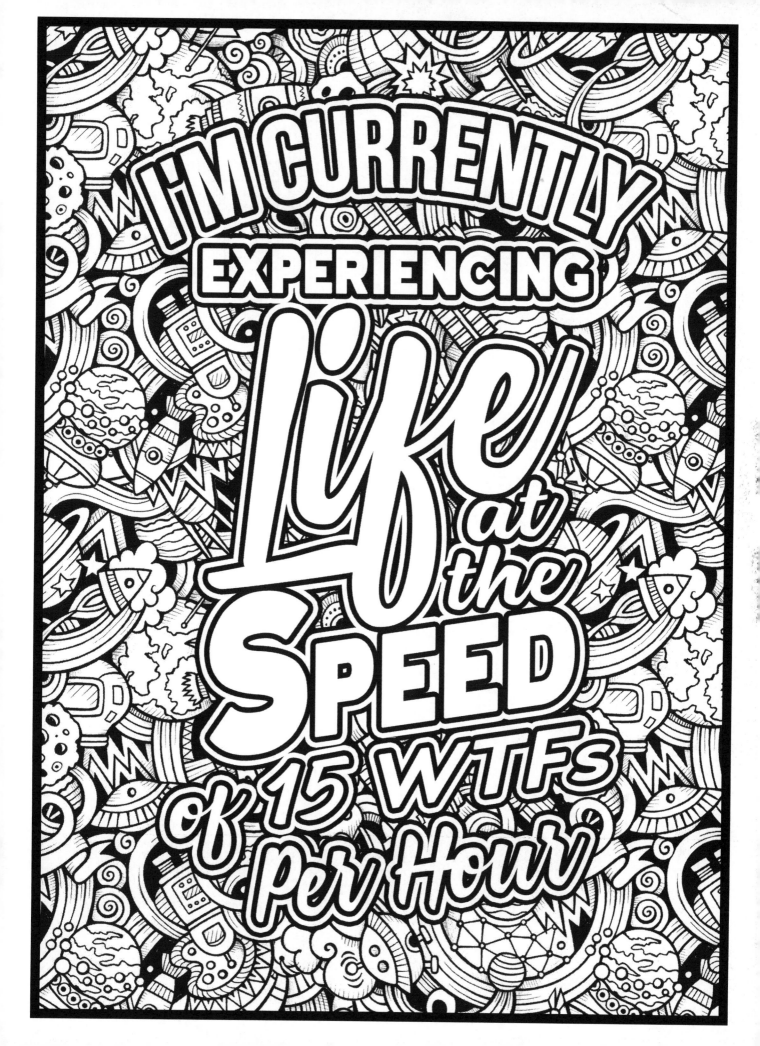

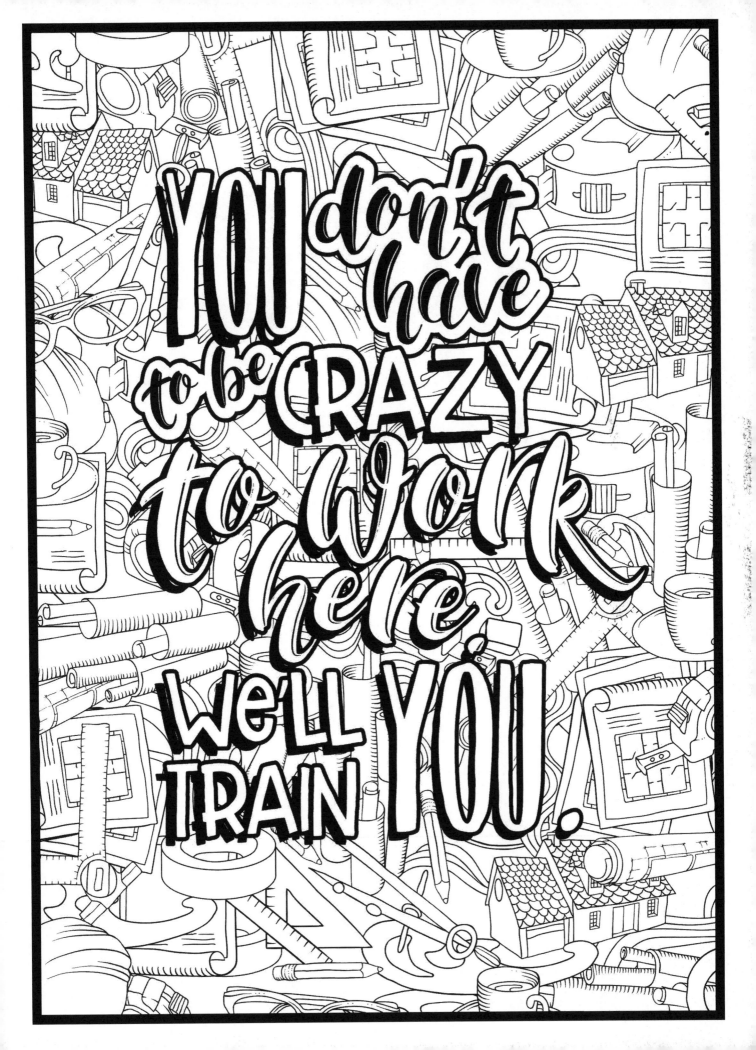

Happiness is not Having to SET an alarm for TOMORROW

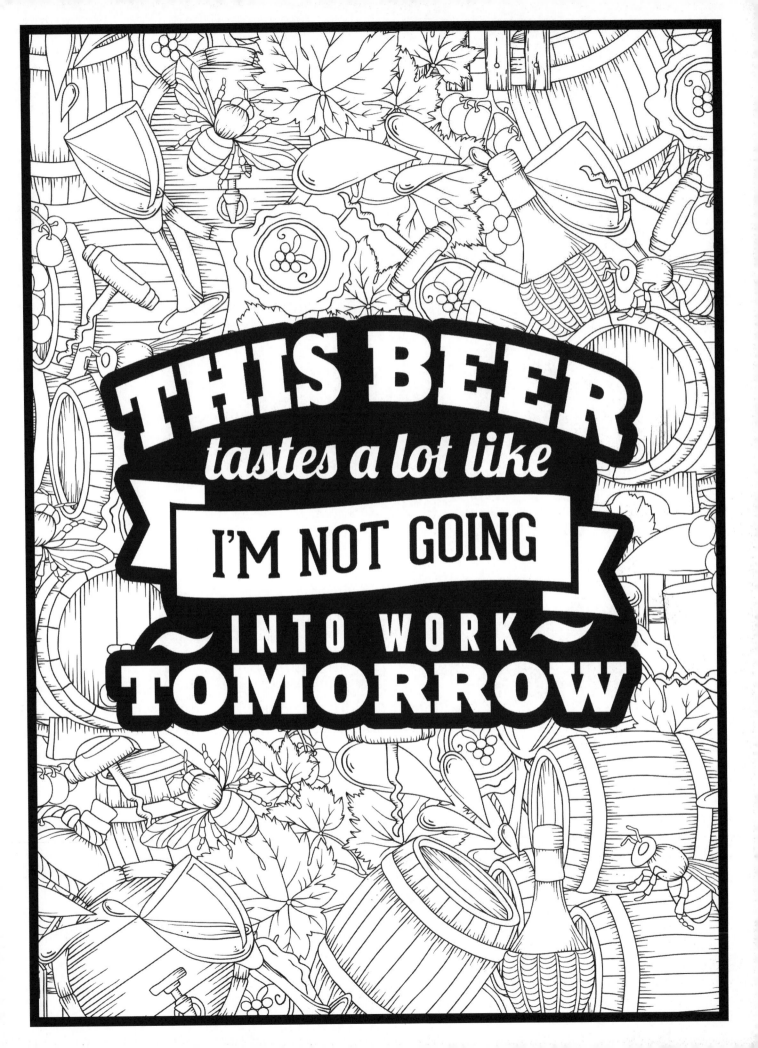

SORRY, BUT YOUR PASSWORD MUST CONTAIN
A SYMBOL, A NUMBER, AN UPPERCASE LETTER,
a HIEROGLYPH
A HAIKU
and THE BLOOD of a VIRGIN

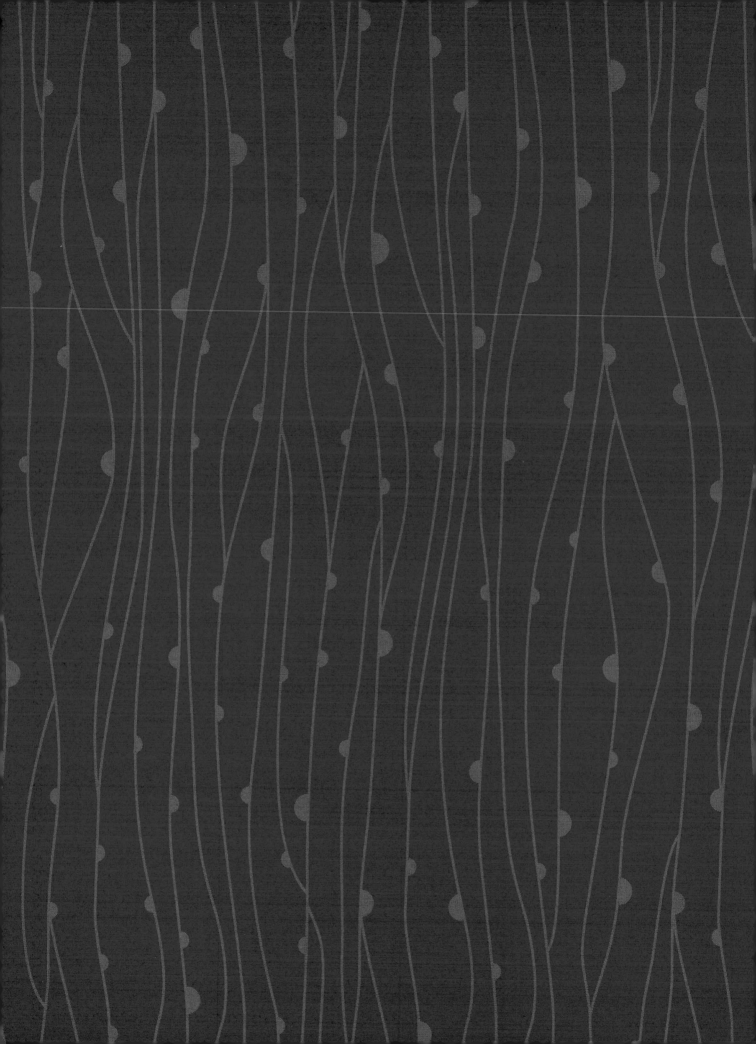

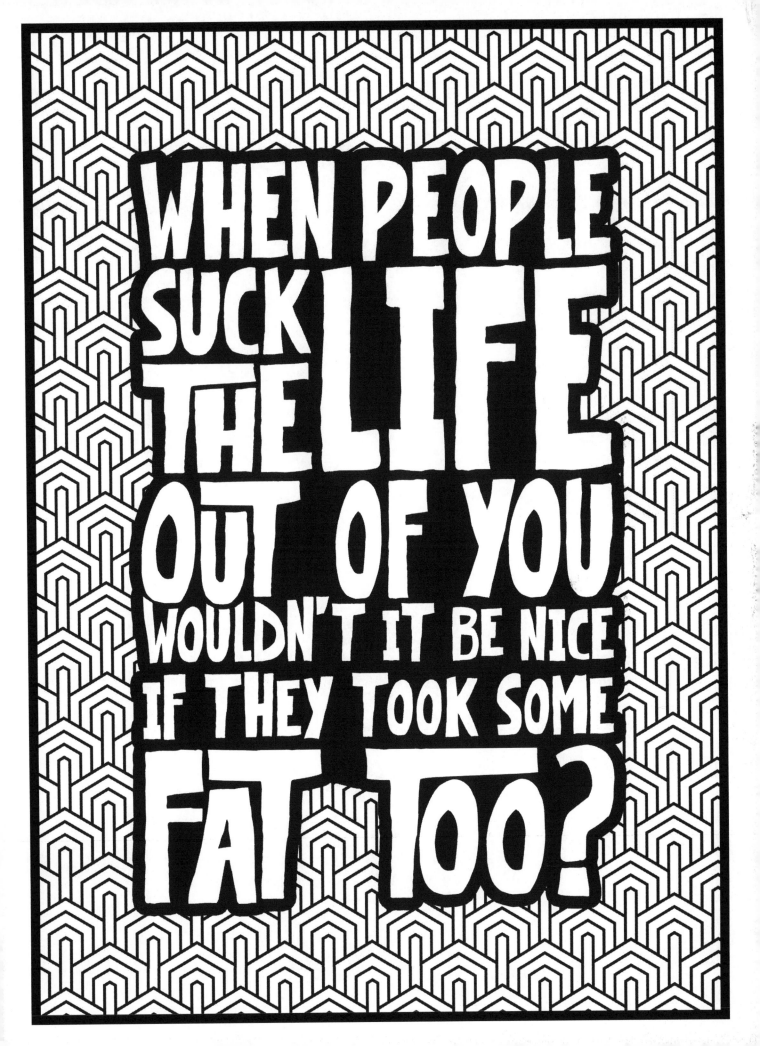

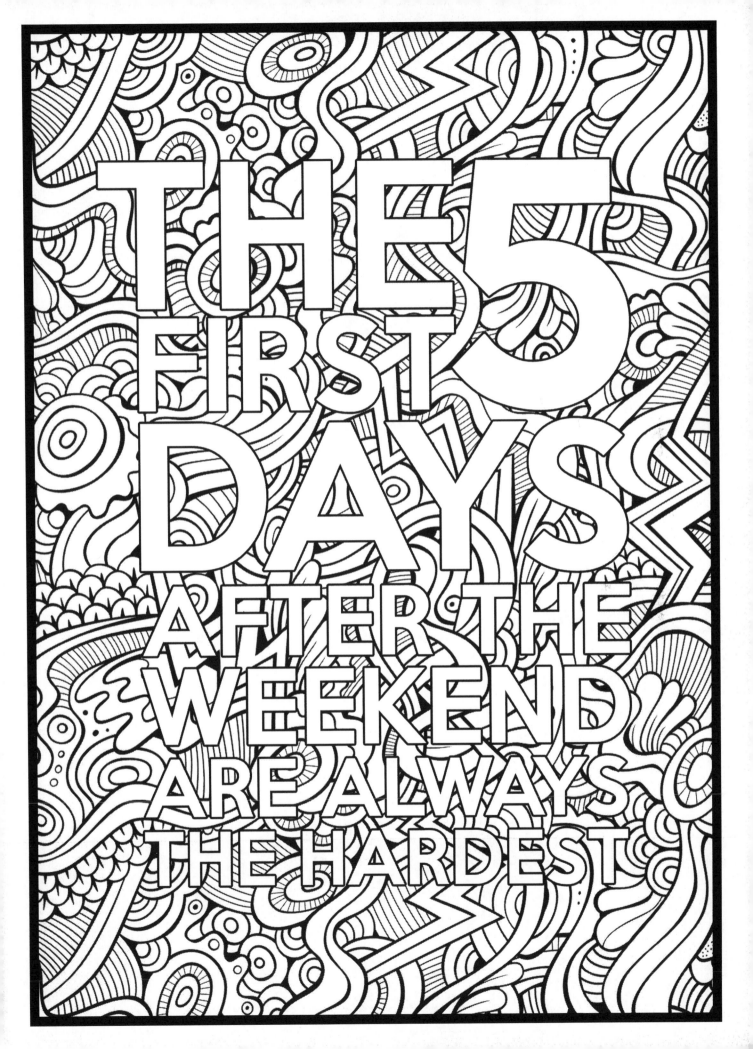

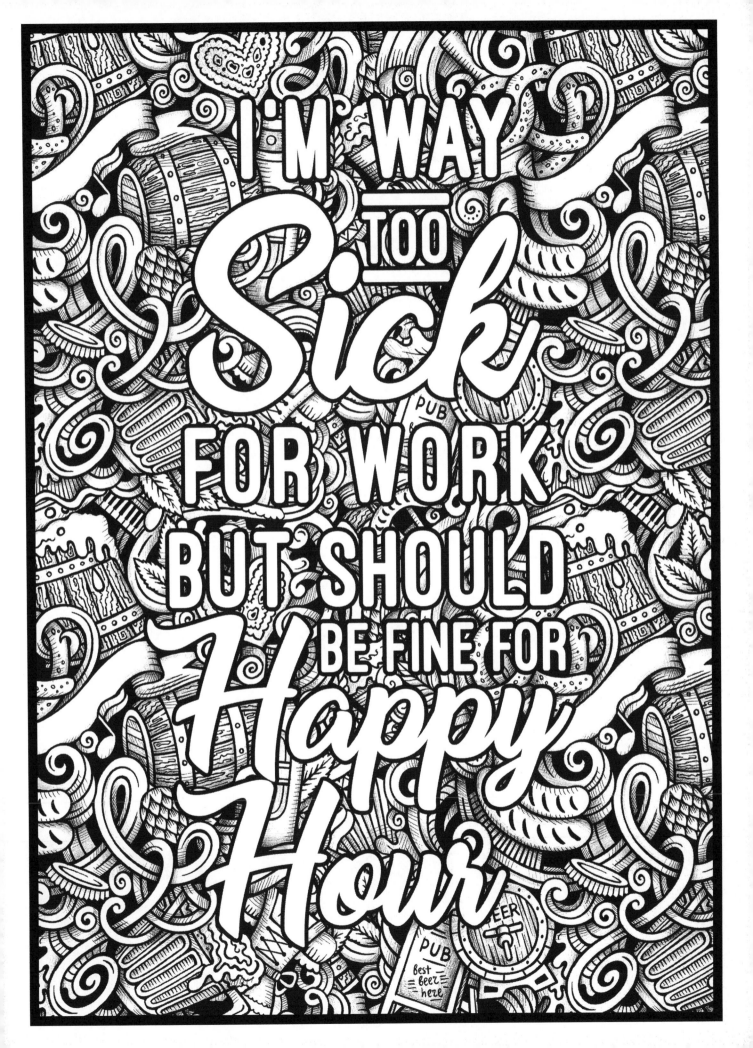

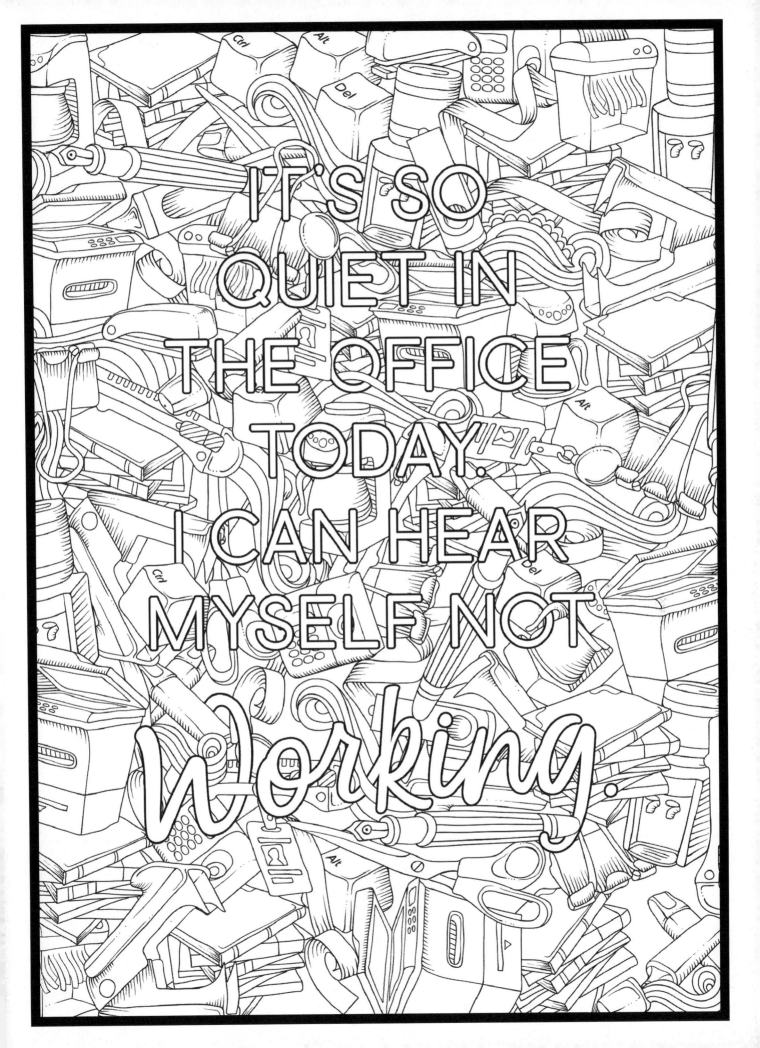

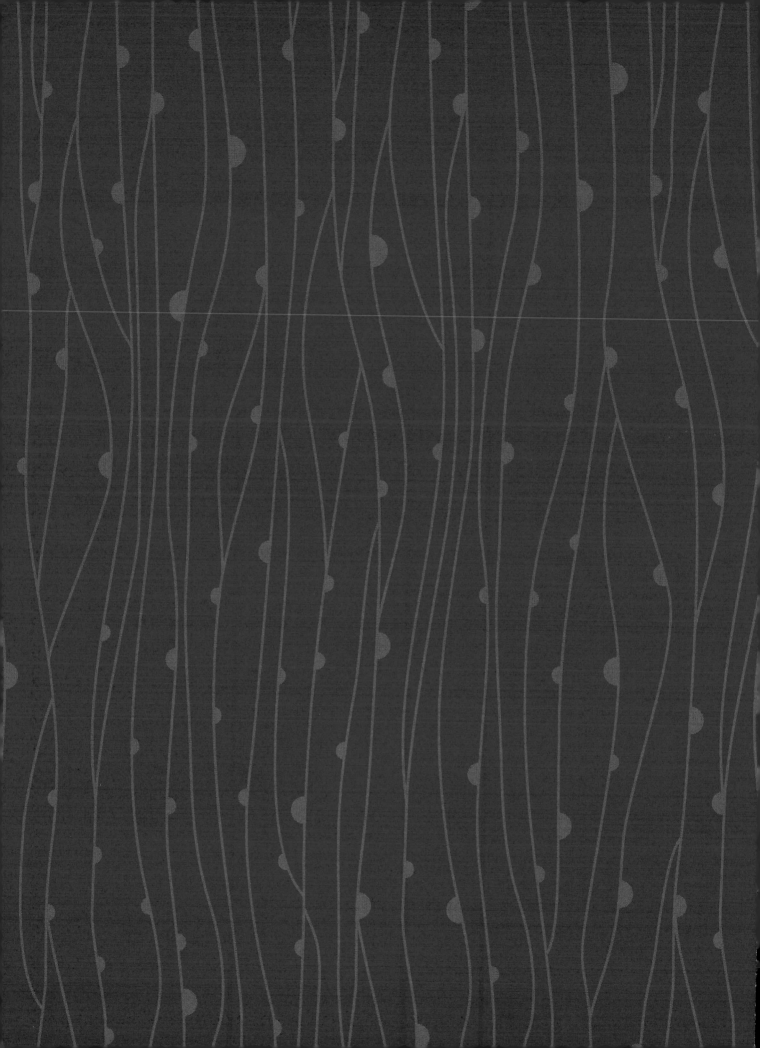

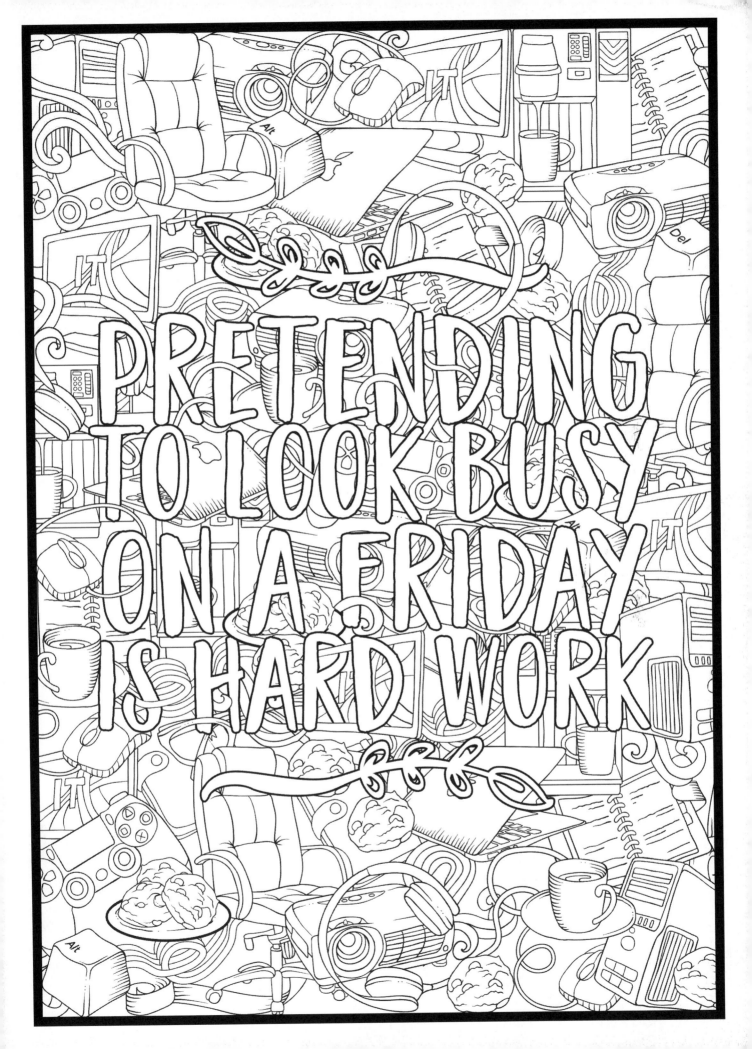

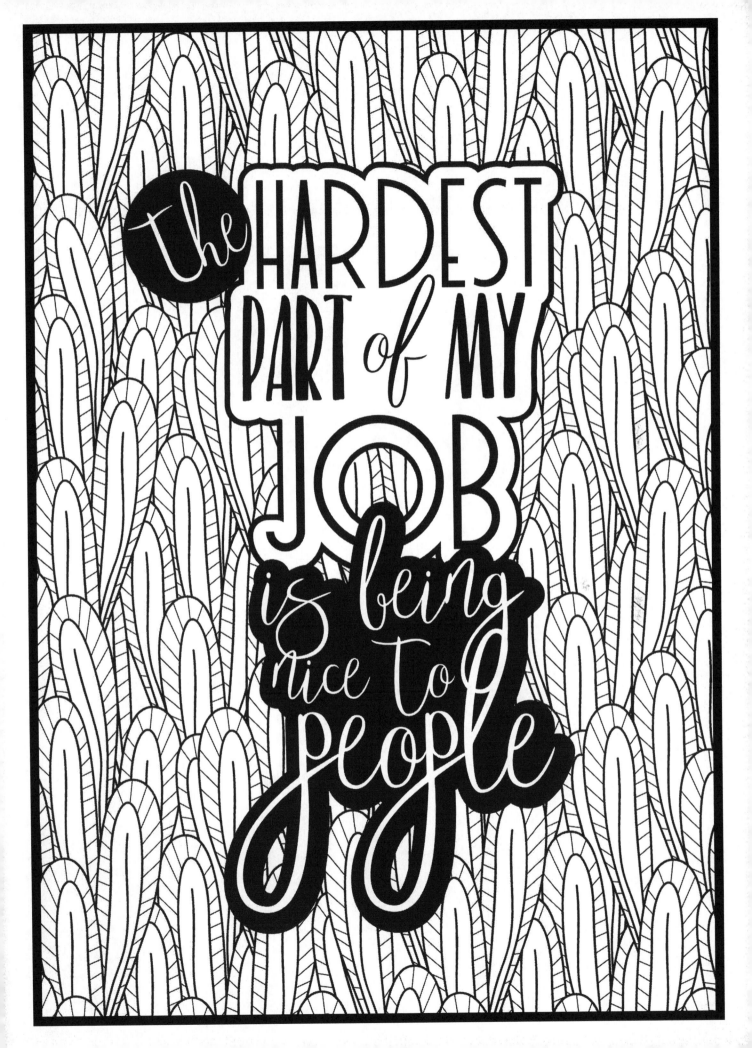

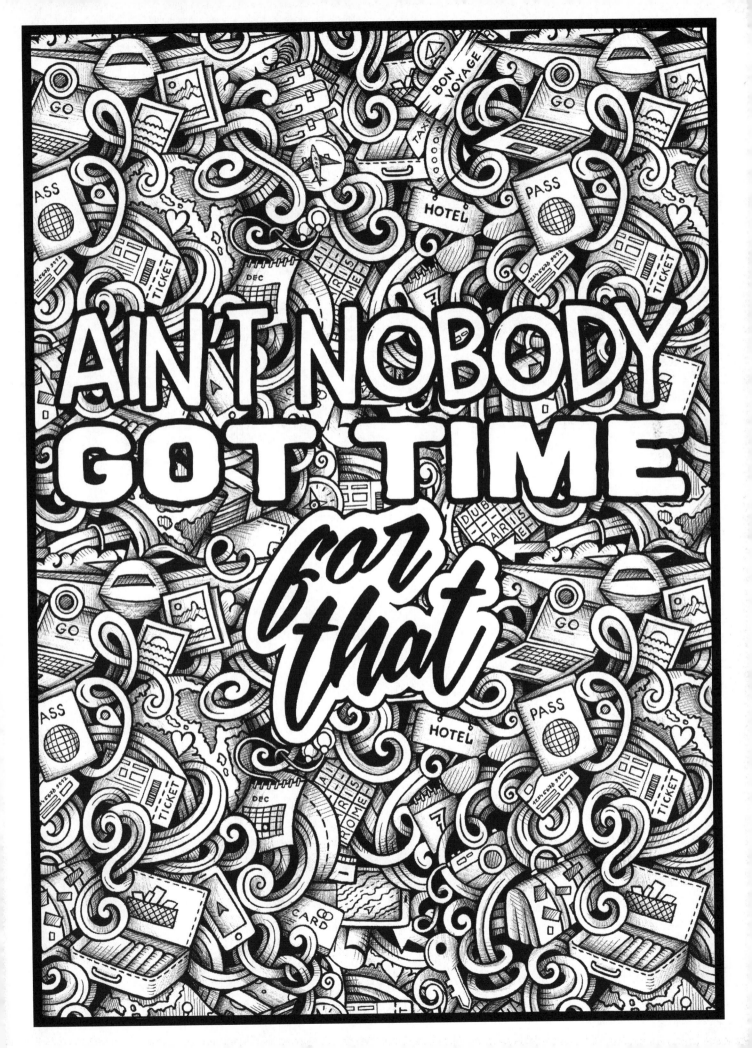

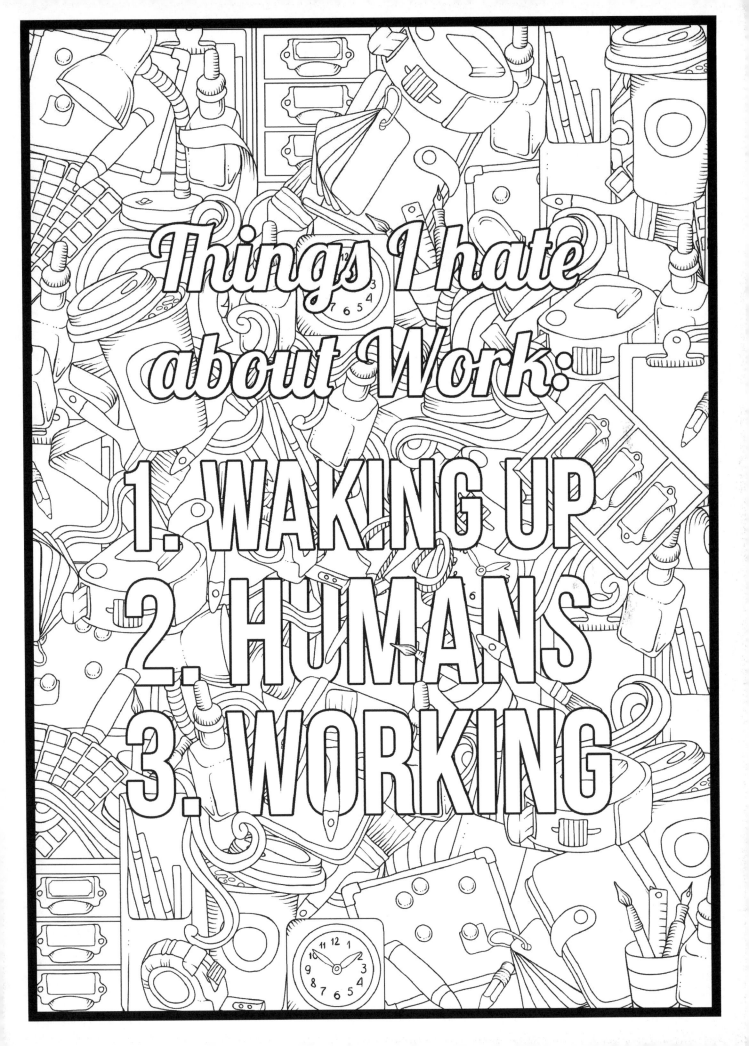

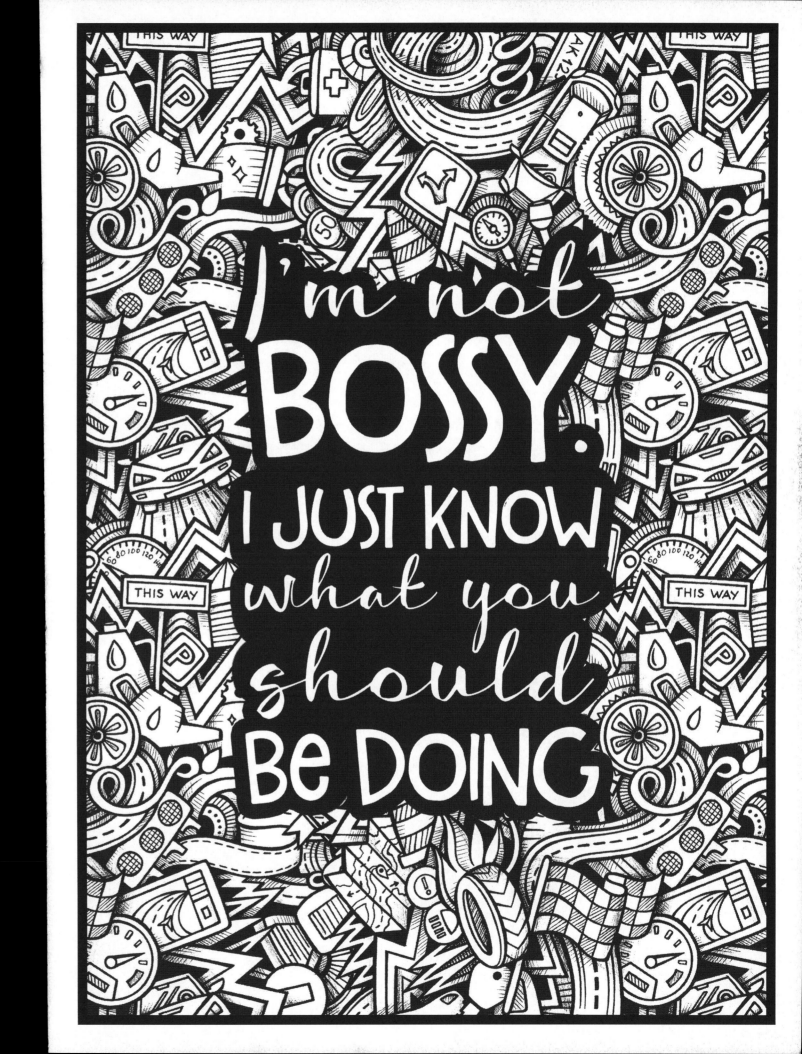

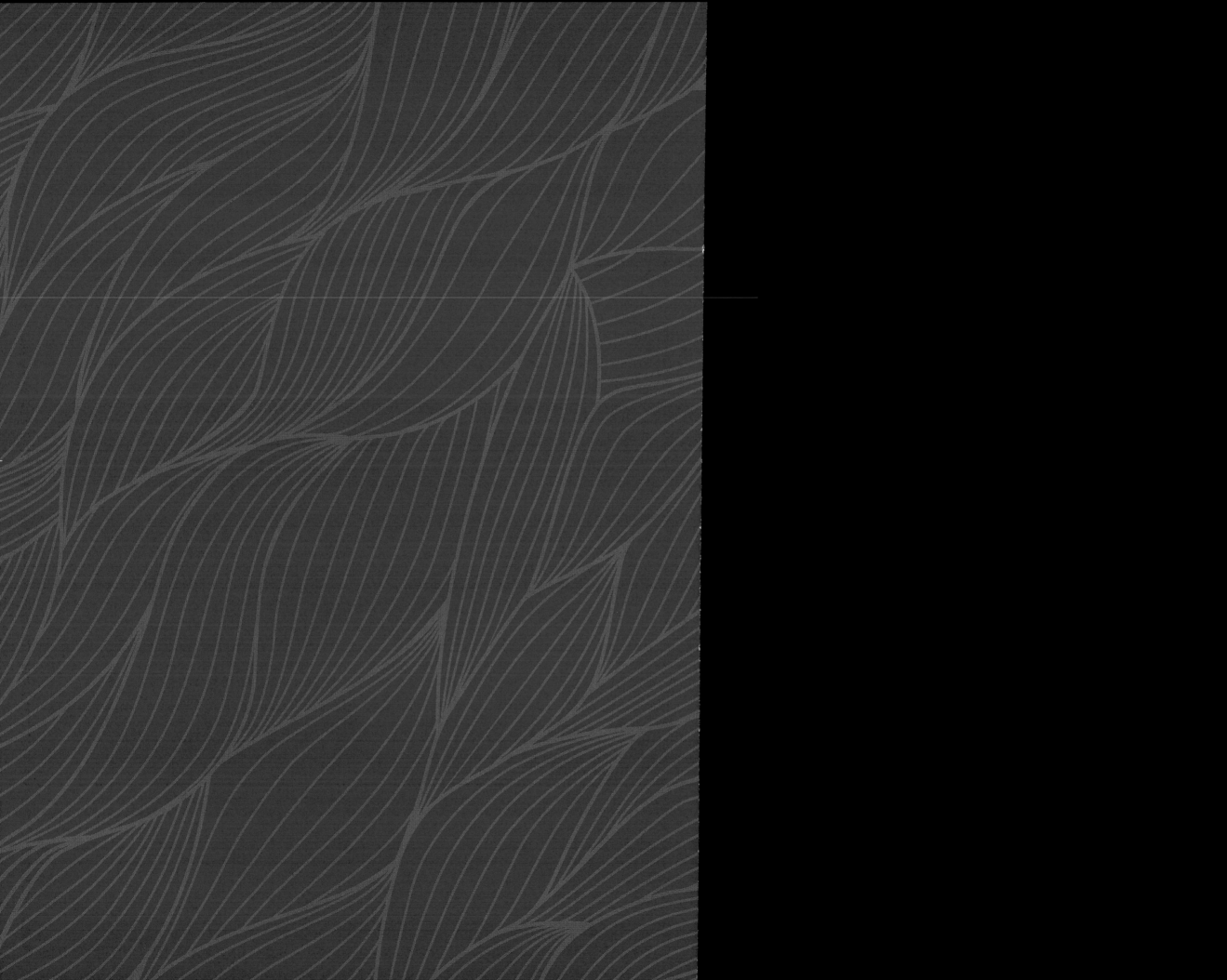

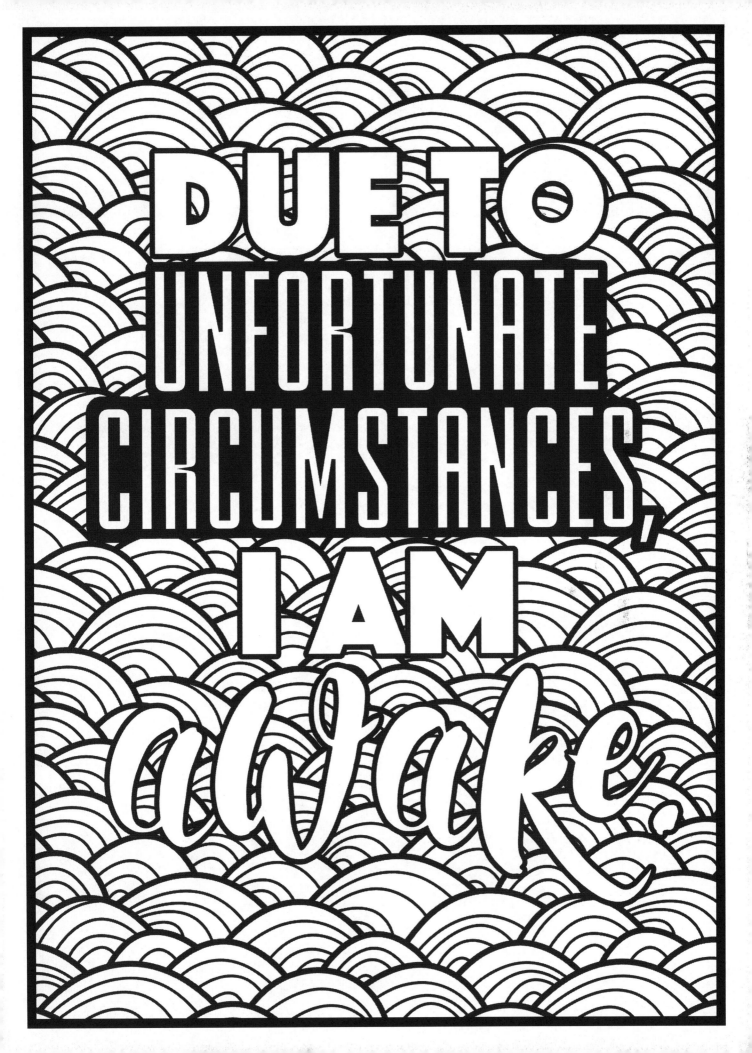

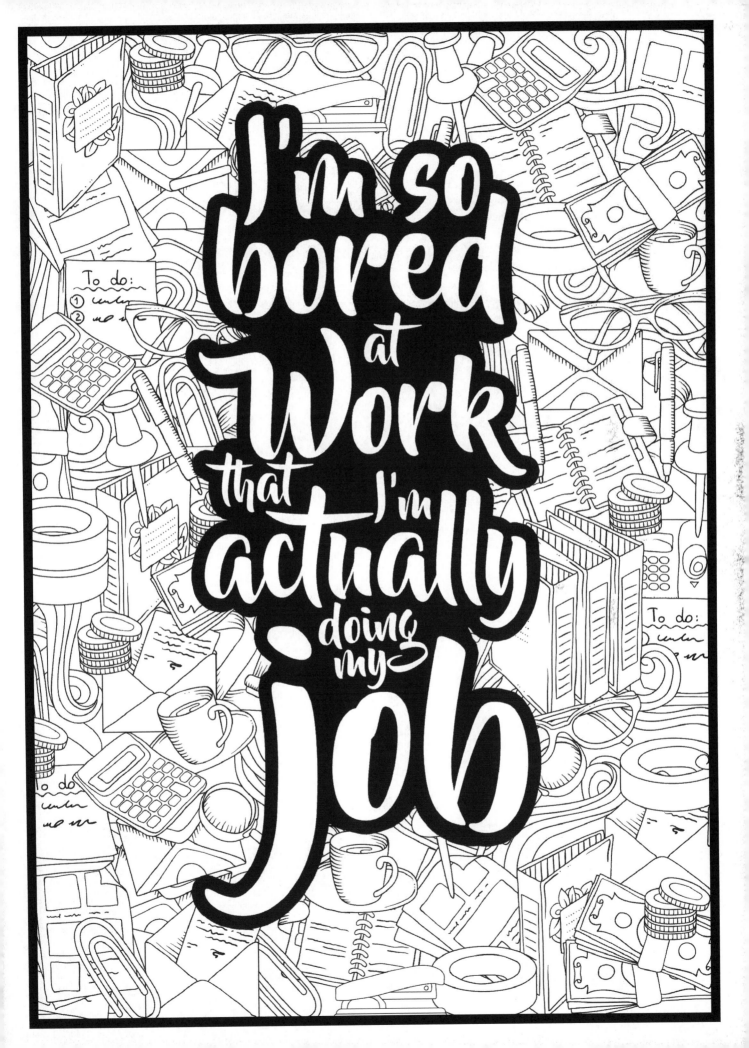

I'VE SEEN MONKEY FECES
FIGHTS AT THE ZOO

MORE
Organized
THAN MY
WORKPLACE!

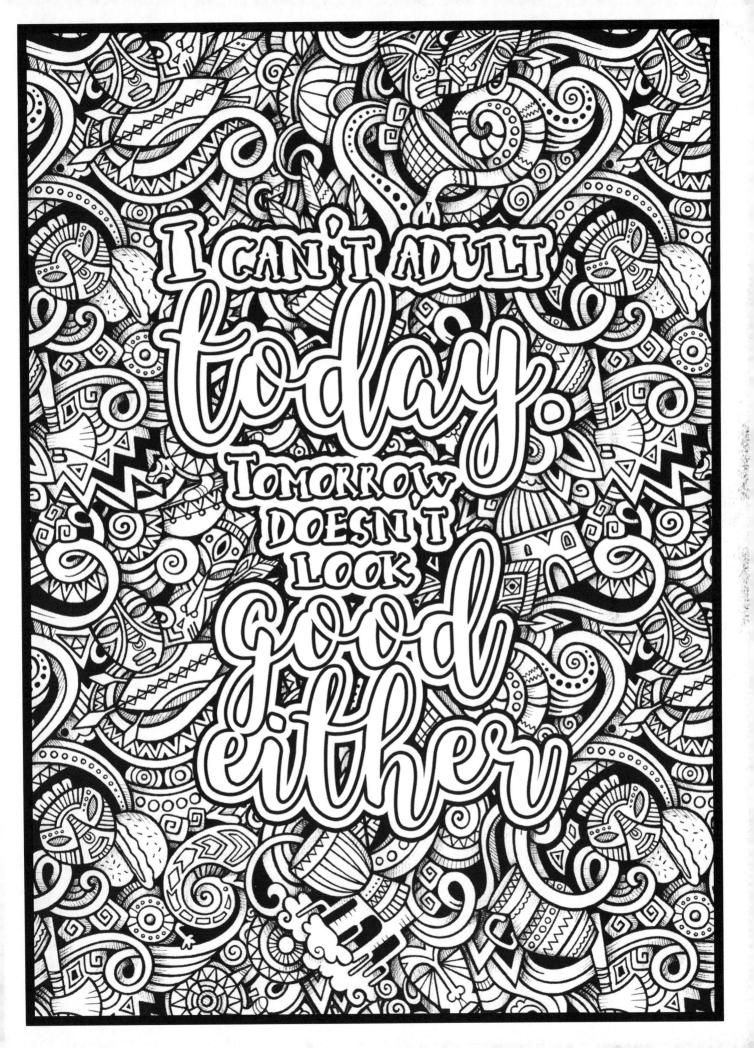

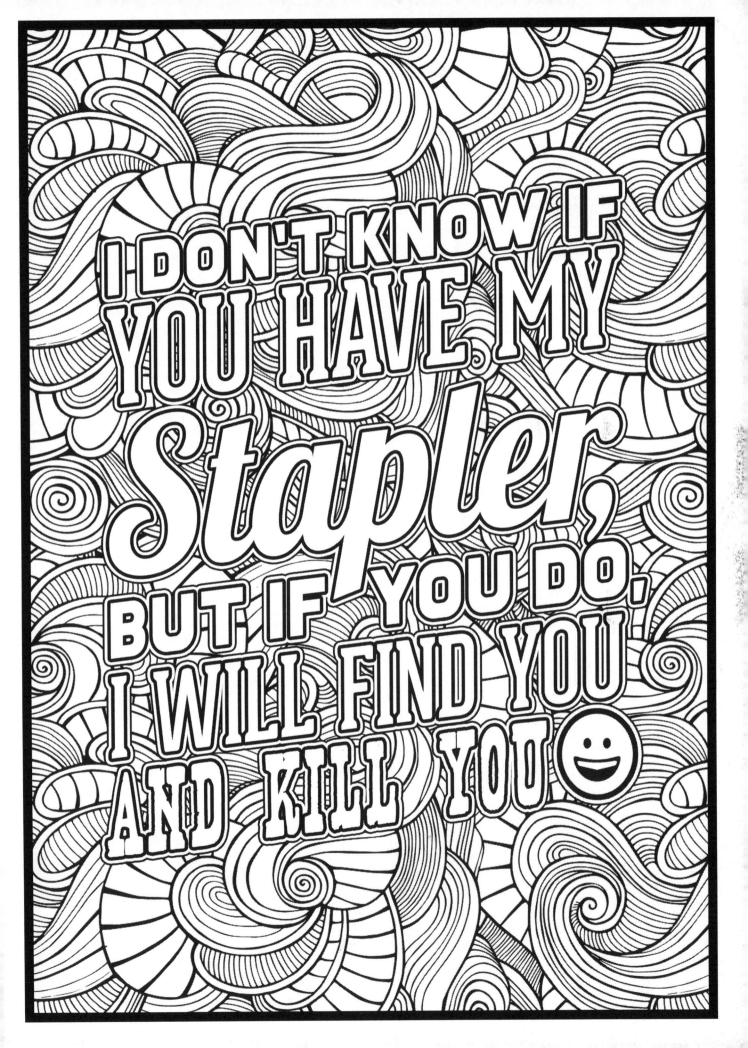

Want free goodies?
Email us at freebies@pbleu.com

@papeteriebleu

Papeterie Bleu

Shop our other books at
www.pbleu.com

Wholesale distribution through Ingram Content Group
www.ingramcontent.com/publishers/distribution/wholesale

For questions and customer service, email us at
support@pbleu.com

Made in the USA
Columbia, SC
03 December 2019

84304540R00061